Original title:
Snowfall Glow

Copyright © 2024 Swan Charm
All rights reserved.

Author: Sara Säde
ISBN HARDBACK: 978-9916-79-633-7
ISBN PAPERBACK: 978-9916-79-634-4
ISBN EBOOK: 978-9916-79-635-1

Celestial Whispers

Stars twinkle softly, a lullaby glow,
Dreams take flight where night breezes flow.
Moonlight kisses shadows with grace,
In this vast cosmos, we find our place.

Galaxies spin in a dance so divine,
Echoes of stardust in pathways align.
Shooting stars whisper secrets untold,
In the silence of night, our hopes unfold.

Frost-Linked Hearts

Winter's breath paints the world pure white,
Frozen branches glimmer in soft twilight.
Footsteps crunch on the carpet of snow,
Hearts beat warm in the cold's gentle flow.

Beneath the moon's watch, promises freeze,
Each glance, a spark, in the chill of the breeze.
Wrapped in warmth under blankets we hide,
Together we glow, like flames side by side.

Quiet Glimmer

In the hushed stillness, a soft light ignites,
Whispers of hope fill the long, quiet nights.
Flickers of courage in shadows cast wide,
Guiding our paths as we walk side by side.

In the morning dew, dreams shimmer and gleam,
Life's gentle melody flows like a stream.
Each moment a treasure, subtle yet bright,
In the heart of silence, we find our light.

Winter's Ethereal Canvas

Snowflakes dance down, a delicate art,
Each one unique, like the beat of a heart.
Trees donned in white, a magical sight,
Nature's still splendor, wrapped snugly at night.

Frozen rivers reflect the moon's soft embrace,
Time stands still in this tranquil space.
With each breath taken, the world holds its breath,
In winter's grasp, we find beauty in depth.

Ethereal Constellation

Stars whisper secrets in the night,
Dreams take flight, pure delight.
A tapestry woven with silver thread,
Guiding wanderers, where they tread.

Galaxies dance in cosmic embrace,
Timeless tales in endless space.
Celestial bodies, a radiant glow,
Painting the dark with a gentle flow.

Moonlight flickers like a distant star,
Illuminating paths from afar.
In the stillness, the universe sighs,
A symphony heard in the skies.

Hearts entwined beneath a veil,
Of stardust, wishes, and a ship's sail.
Journeying through this midnight sea,
Together forever, just you and me.

In the quiet, let our spirits soar,
Bound by love, we seek evermore.
Ethereal moments, a precious find,
In the constellation of the mind.

Frigid Glow

Beneath the chill, a soft light glows,
Illuminating paths where the cold wind blows.
Frosted branches, a shimmering sight,
Nature's beauty in the deep of night.

Snowflakes dance like tiny stars,
Whispering dreams of distant Mars.
Each flake unique, a fleeting grace,
In the silence, an embrace takes place.

Frost-kissed air, sharp and clear,
Echoes of laughter, family near.
Warmth radiates from hearts aglow,
In winter's grasp, our spirits grow.

Candles flicker in the deepening dusk,
Filling the room with peace and trust.
Frigid echoes held by love's fire,
Kindling hope, lifting us higher.

Under the stars, together we glow,
Finding warmth in the cold below.
Frigid landscapes may steal the show,
Yet warmth resides where hearts choose to go.

Veiled in Ice

Silent whispers in the winter air,
Secrets hidden, a fragile snare.
Worlds encased in a crystal sheath,
Veiled in ice, where dreams breathe.

Frozen rivers dance with grace,
Mirroring clouds in a soft embrace.
Nature shimmers, a diamond's light,
Time slows down in the heart of night.

Every branch wears a frosted crown,
As the sun dips low, painting the town.
Light refracts through the icy veil,
Revealing stories in every trail.

A chilling beauty, haunting and deep,
In this stillness, the world seems to sleep.
Under layers of frost, life remains,
Veiled in silence, yet it contains.

With every breath, we warm the air,
In winter's hold, we find our share.
Veiled in ice, our hearts ignite,
Unraveling wonders in the moonlight.

Frosted Luminosity

In the dawn's light, the world takes pause,
Frosted surfaces, nature's cause.
Glistening like diamonds in the sky,
Stories whispered from days gone by.

Icicles hang, sharp and bright,
Nature's art, a stunning sight.
Twinkling shadows dance on the ground,
In this moment, peace is found.

Gentle breath of the morning chill,
Frosted petals, a silent thrill.
Each layer wraps the earth so tight,
Cloaked in beauty, bathed in light.

The sun awakes, painting gold,
Unveiling the secrets that winter holds.
In this quiet, hearts unite,
Frosted luminosity, pure and bright.

Together we walk, hand in hand,
Through fields of ice, across the land.
In the morning glow, hope will rise,
Frosted visions in winter skies.

Twinkling Threads of Chill

In the quiet night they gleam,
Silver threads weave through the dream.
Whispers soft in frosty air,
Each one beckons with a stare.

Journey on the winter's breath,
Silent tales of life and death.
Stars above like gems so bright,
Guide us gently through the night.

Beneath the moon's pale embrace,
Nature's beauty dresses space.
Gentle sighs of snowy trees,
Carried forth upon the breeze.

Frosted patterns dress the ground,
In their charm, peace can be found.
With each step, a crisp delight,
Footprints lost in soft twilight.

Threads of chill, a dance of light,
Woven peace in winter's night.
Each reflection plays its part,
In the tapestry of heart.

Frosted Lanterns in the Dark

Frosted lanterns line the street,
Casting shadows at our feet.
Glimmers dance on icy glass,
In the night, hours quickly pass.

Each light holds a tale untold,
In their glow, warmth against the cold.
They flicker soft, a guiding spark,
Illuminating pathways dark.

Gentle whispers fill the air,
Stories woven, moments rare.
Underneath the starry dome,
Every heart finds its true home.

A path adorned with light's embrace,
Follows hope through time and space.
Frosted lanterns shining bright,
Banish fears and bring forth light.

In their glow, we start to dream,
Life's adventures softly beam.
Through the dark, we drift along,
Chasing echoes, finding song.

Luminary Silence

In the stillness of the night,
Stars emerge, a tranquil sight.
Silence deep, a soothing balm,
Cradles whispers, brings us calm.

Fleeting thoughts drift through the void,
In the quiet, fears destroyed.
Illuminated by their grace,
Peaceful moments find their place.

Time stands still, the world asleep,
Into dreams we softly seep.
Each twinkling light, a quiet guide,
Illuminates the paths we bide.

A canvas of the night unfurled,
Holding secrets of the world.
In this hush, our souls unite,
Breath of life, the stars ignite.

In luminary silence found,
Hearts awaken, souls unbound.
In the darkness, truths arise,
Painting stories in the skies.

Icy Stardust

Whispers of the night unfold,
Icy stardust, stories told.
Scattered gems upon the ground,
In their grace, enchantment's found.

Like the dance of falling snow,
Sparkling trails where cold winds blow.
Each a wish, a hope to keep,
In the quiet, secrets leap.

Glimmers pass like fleeting dreams,
Caught in moonlight's silver beams.
Stardust drapes the sleeping earth,
Warming tales of love and birth.

Beneath the cosmos' watchful eye,
Connections flare as spirits fly.
Icy fragments, glistening light,
Guide us through the velvet night.

Icy stardust fills the air,
Merging souls in wonder's stare.
With each breath, new stories weave,
In the glow, we learn to believe.

Hushed Hypothermia

Silent whispers in the night,
Chill envelops, stars are bright.
Frosty breath in the calm air,
Nature sleeps without a care.

Beneath the moon's soft silver glow,
Silent shadows dance below.
The world covered in icy lace,
Dreams unfold in this still space.

Crystalline peace wraps the trees,
Echoes carried on the breeze.
Time is frozen, moments pass,
Underneath this frozen glass.

A stillness wraps around the ground,
In this quiet, thoughts abound.
Embers fade from warmth's embrace,
Hushed in wintry, soft embrace.

As dawn breaks with softest light,
Hope awakens, ends the night.
Hushed hypothermia's sweet song,
Inviting all who wander long.

Celestial Powder

Twinkle in the velvet sky,
Sparkling bliss as dreams fly high.
Meteors trace their fiery path,
Whispers echo in their wrath.

A sprinkle of the stars above,
Scattering magic, purest love.
Galaxies swirl in endless dance,
In a cosmic, timeless trance.

Celestial powder on my skin,
Draped in wonder, I begin.
Every wish finds its way home,
In this universe, I freely roam.

Nebulas bloom in colors bright,
Celestial hues bask in light.
Through the cosmos, we will glide,
On dreams, we cannot hide.

With each breath, the universe sings,
Carving pathways through our wings.
Celestial powder, constellations,
Fueling the heart's aspirations.

Frosted Fantasia

In a world of shimmering white,
Frosted dreams dance in the light.
Every crystal holds a tale,
Of winter's charm, soft and frail.

Trees adorned with sparkling frost,
Beauty captured, never lost.
Nature weaves a wondrous sight,
In the hush of frosty night.

Snowflakes twirl like fairies sweet,
Gracefully they kiss my feet.
In this realm of icy grace,
Magic glimmers in each space.

Whispers carried on the breeze,
Songs of winter, calm and ease.
In this frosted fantasy land,
Joy and peace go hand in hand.

Every moment feels profound,
In this beauty all around.
Frosted hopes, a heart that sings,
In the joy that winter brings.

Glimmering Expanse

Beyond the horizon, dreams awake,
A glimmering expanse, a chance to take.
Waves of light ripple through the air,
In this vastness, I'm aware.

Every star a distant guide,
In this journey, I confide.
Moments stretch, the world in view,
Endless sky, in shades of blue.

Horizons blend in colors bright,
As day retreats to greet the night.
The universe whispers, soft and low,
Signaling paths I long to know.

Around me, echoes of the past,
Memories shimmer, hold me fast.
With every heartbeat, I expand,
In this glimmering, wondrous land.

Adventure calls in shadows deep,
In this expanse, secrets keep.
With open heart, I'll venture far,
Guided by my wishing star.

Heavenly Frost

Crystal flakes in quiet flight,
Whisper soft, embrace the night.
Nature wears a cloak of grace,
In this calm, a sacred space.

Branches bend with diamond tears,
Stillness hushes all our fears.
Underneath the moon's soft gaze,
Winter glows in silver haze.

Footsteps crunch on frosty ground,
Magic lives in sights profound.
Every breath a cloud of white,
In the chill, all hearts unite.

Stars are born from icy dreams,
Shimmering like sunlight beams.
In this realm of purest light,
We find solace in the night.

Nature's breath, a frozen song,
In its stillness, we belong.
Heavenly frost paints the dawn,
A new day waits, quietly drawn.

Hushed in White

Blankets spread across the land,
A gentle touch, a soft command.
Hushed in white, the world does sleep,
Secrets in the snow, they keep.

Footprints fade beneath the skies,
Underneath the frosty sighs.
In this silence, hearts entwine,
Finding peace in every line.

Icicles hang like frozen dreams,
Caught in daylight's silver beams.
Nature's breath, a frosty kiss,
In this moment, purest bliss.

Whispers travel on the breeze,
Through the branches of the trees.
Hushed in white, we walk as one,
Until the day is gently done.

Stars will sparkle, skies will shine,
In this quiet, love is mine.
Hushed in white, forevermore,
In the silence, hearts explore.

Glazed Wilderness

Branches draped in icy lace,
Nature dons a frozen face.
Glazed wilderness, stark and bold,
In its beauty, stories told.

Footprints lead through crystal scenes,
Where the silence grows between.
Every twig a work of art,
In this realm, we share a heart.

Frozen rivers gently glide,
Mirroring the world outside.
Life finds ways in winter's chill,
With a quiet, steadfast will.

Beneath the stars, the silence reigns,
In the stillness, joy remains.
Nature whispers secrets low,
Glazed wilderness, purest glow.

Amidst the frost, a fire burns,
For the beauty, nature yearns.
Through the chill, we wander free,
Finding warmth in harmony.

Shimmering Silence

Amidst the snowflakes, time stands still,
A soft embrace, a hopeful thrill.
Shimmering silence breaks the night,
In the glow, everything feels right.

Every breath, a cloud of white,
Filling hearts with pure delight.
Stars above, like diamonds shine,
Guiding souls in paths divine.

In the stillness, we find peace,
A gentle beauty that won't cease.
Nature hums a lullaby,
Underneath the winter sky.

As the world wraps up in dreams,
Life is woven with silent seams.
Shimmering silence wraps us tight,
In its arms, we find the light.

Night unfolds with whispered grace,
In the stillness, we find our place.
Shimmering silence all around,
In this moment, love is found.

Glistening Silence

In the quiet night, stars gleam bright,
Snowflakes whisper, pure delight.
Moonlight spills over the ground,
In this stillness, peace is found.

Footsteps crunch on the snowy crust,
Breath like clouds, in the night we trust.
Nature holds its breath, serene,
Wrapped in the magic, softly seen.

Each flake falls with careful grace,
Time slows down in this tranquil space.
Hearts beat softly, dreams take flight,
Lost in this glistening, silent night.

A world transformed by winter's art,
Peaceful moments we hold to heart.
In this silence, we find our way,
Embraced by night, till break of day.

Let the shadows dance and sway,
As we linger, hearts at play.
In gleaming silence, truth we find,
Together in the stillness, aligned.

Midnight Flurries

The clock strikes twelve, the world aglow,
Midnight flurries begin to flow.
Tiny dancers grace the air,
Twisting, turning, without a care.

A frosty breeze whispers low,
As snowflakes fall, a soft halo.
Each one unique, a fleeting art,
Carving beauty, they steal the heart.

Under the moon's pale embrace,
Winter's charm sets a brisk pace.
The night alive with whispered dreams,
In the flurries, magic beams.

Time melts gently, slipping fast,
Moments captured, forever cast.
Together we share this winter's song,
In the midnight flurries, we belong.

So let's cherish this time so rare,
As the world transforms with every air,
In the heart of night, we dance and twirl,
Embraced by snow, in dreams we swirl.

A Dance of Light

Softly glowing, the dawn breaks clear,
Light spills gently, drawing near.
Dancing shadows, a playful sight,
The world awakens in colors bright.

Golden rays through the branches weave,
A tapestry of hope we conceive.
Sunlight kisses the dewy grass,
In this moment, worries pass.

Nature sways in a vibrant song,
Where the heart feels it belongs.
Every leaf, a shimmering kite,
In the breeze, a dance of light.

With each whisper, the day ignites,
Painting the world in dazzling sights.
A ballet of warmth, both near and far,
Guided by the morning star.

As the sun climbs, shadows recede,
Nature's beauty, our souls feed.
In this dance, our spirits rise,
A symphony under endless skies.

Frosted Embrace

Winter wraps the world so tight,
In a frosted embrace, pure and white.
Chill in the air, crisp and bold,
Whispers of stories, timelessly told.

Each branch dressed in delicate frost,
In the season's dance, never lost.
Silent nights blanket the earth,
Moments of magic, quiet mirth.

Fires crackle, warmth aglow,
While outside, gentle winds blow.
We gather close, hearts entwined,
In this frosted embrace, we find.

Snowflakes twirl, a soft ballet,
In winter's arms, we choose to stay.
Under stars that shimmer with grace,
Lost together in this warm space.

So let us cherish this time so dear,
As the frost brings us near.
In a world of wonder, gently trace,
The beauty found in a frosted embrace.

Gleaming Drift

Softly falls the winter's snow,
A blanket pure, a shimmering glow.
Footsteps crunch on frosty ground,
In silent woods, peace can be found.

Glistening trees in silver light,
Whispers echo through the night.
Moonlit paths where shadows play,
A dreamlike world, we drift away.

Stars above like diamonds shine,
In this moment, hearts align.
Drifting thoughts on chilly air,
Hope and wonder everywhere.

Nature sleeps in soft embrace,
Time stands still in this vast space.
Breathe in deep, let worries cease,
In the drift, we find our peace.

Frosty Reverie

Morning breaks with frosty breath,
A canvas white, the world in quest.
Each flake dances, unique in grace,
Painting beauty on nature's face.

Winter's chill wraps all in dreams,
Whispers soft like gentle streams.
Footprints mark a fleeting trace,
In this frozen, magic place.

Branches bare in crystal dress,
Nature's pause, a tranquil press.
In the stillness, thoughts take flight,
Underneath the pale moonlight.

Time drifts slow as shadows play,
Clouds of white drift far away.
In the frosty realms we share,
Love and warmth linger in the air.

Luminous Chill

The night unfolds with stars aglow,
A luminous chill from sands of snow.
Silent winds weave through the trees,
Carrying whispers on the breeze.

Glowing moon in skies so high,
Casts a light where shadows lie.
Each moment captured, crystal clear,
In the stillness, hope draws near.

Frosted breath, a fleeting sigh,
Painting dreams that softly fly.
In this realm of quiet grace,
Time slows down, we find our place.

Luminous whispers fill the night,
A dance of dreams, pure delight.
In the chill, our hearts unite,
In this glow, love feels so right.

Shining White Whispers

In the twilight, snowflakes fall,
Softly weaving nature's call.
Bright and white, a tender glow,
Whispers echo through the snow.

Pines adorned in shining light,
Stand like sentinels in night.
A tranquil hush embraces all,
In this stillness, we hear the call.

Footsteps lead to paths unknown,
In this world, no seeds are sown.
Yet in wonder, hearts expand,
Together, we still take a stand.

Each flake dances, a gentle waltz,
In this moment, we find our faults.
But wrapped in love and whispered grace,
We light the dark, we find our place.

Charmed by the Winter Light

Soft whispers glow in evening's grace,
As shadows dance with a gentle pace.
Winter's breath in twilight sings,
A magic born of frost-tipped wings.

Stars adorn the velvet sky,
While silver flakes begin to fly.
In this realm of quiet dreams,
Hope unfurls in sparkling streams.

Beneath the weight of purest snow,
Hearts awaken, warmth to flow.
Embraced by stillness, love ignites,
Charmed forever by winter's lights.

The world adorned in glistening white,
Crafts moments pure, the spirit's flight.
Each breath a cloud, a fleeting sight,
In winter's arms, we find delight.

Upturned Sky of Frost

Underneath the endless dome,
Where frozen stars begin to roam.
Each breath a hue, each glance a spark,
We wander softly through the dark.

Crystals twinkle on the trees,
Nature's art in winter's breeze.
Frosty kisses on our cheeks,
In this wonder, solace speaks.

Shadows linger, stories unfold,
Whispered tales of nights so bold.
Underneath this frosted sky,
Dreams take flight, they soar and fly.

With every step, a tale anew,
The world transformed in silver hue.
In every corner, magic lies,
Underneath these upturned skies.

Velvet Luminescence

Night descends with a silken touch,
A world aglow, it means so much.
Stars emerge like seeds of light,
Dancing softly, breaking night.

Every flake a story told,
Whispers of the brave and bold.
In this quilt of dreams we spin,
Velvet shadows draw us in.

Moonlight spills on gentle seas,
Fragrant winds bring memories.
In this warmth, our spirits weave,
Together bound, we dare believe.

Captured by the night's embrace,
Lost and found in this vast space.
Luminescent, bright and true,
In velvet dreams, we find our view.

Chill of Enchantment

A breath of air, a frosty veil,
Whispers on the winter trail.
Crunching snow beneath our feet,
A rhythmic echo, soft and sweet.

Glistening in the morning sun,
Nature's dance has just begun.
Underneath the chilled expanse,
Magic swirls in every glance.

Silvery branches gracefully sway,
Enchantments linger, here to stay.
In every corner, whispers rise,
Beneath the chill of morning skies.

Every moment, wrapped in grace,
Time slows down, we find our place.
With every heartbeat, magic flows,
In this chill, enchantment grows.

Whispers of Winter's Light

The frost caresses the silent trees,
Whispers of winter dance on the breeze.
Stars peek through a velvet night,
Echoes of warmth, a soft, glowing light.

Snowflakes twirl in a silent ballet,
Nature sleeps, at the close of day.
Shadows gather beneath the moon,
Winter's breath sings a soothing tune.

Chill in the air, yet hearts feel warm,
Wrapped in peace, away from the storm.
Footprints laid in the fresh white snow,
Tales of the past in the twilight glow.

The night sky shimmers, a diamond sheet,
Each breath released, a clouded retreat.
Under the heavens, dreams take flight,
In whispers soft, winter feels right.

Frosted Dreams Unfold

In the hush of a frosty dawn,
Pastel skies awaken the lawn.
Dreams lie hidden beneath the frost,
Whispers of dawn, never lost.

Glistening branches wear their crowns,
In winter's theater, no one frowns.
Nature's magic, a candid show,
Frosted dreams that softly glow.

Footsteps echo, in the quiet air,
Each moment cherished, so rare.
Life awakens, beneath the white,
A canvas fresh, the world feels bright.

Hope springs from the icy ground,
Resilience shines, beauty is found.
With every breath, the chill ignites,
Frosted dreams unfold in lights.

Silent Radiance

The moon hangs low in a sea of stars,
Night's embrace, veiled in memoirs.
In silence, radiance softly glows,
A tranquil world, where calmness flows.

Each heart beats with a hushed song,
In the stillness, we all belong.
Soft shadows dance on icy ground,
In silent night, beauty is found.

The frost reflects each troubled thought,
A mirrored stillness, lessons taught.
Underneath the silvery light,
Hope reigns strong through the quiet night.

Glistening paths where secrets tread,
In dreams of warmth, no fear or dread.
Within this space, find peace and grace,
A silent radiance in time and place.

Glimmering Tranquility

Stars twinkle softly in the night,
A glimmering path, pure and bright.
In the stillness, calmness grows,
Where the river of quiet flows.

Moonlight dances on the snow,
Whispers of twilight begin to glow.
Peaceful moments fill the air,
Glimmering dreams that hang with care.

Snow-kissed trees stand tall and wise,
Gazing down at the world with sighs.
Nature's embrace, tender and deep,
Lulls the weary souls to sleep.

In the heart of winter's grace,
Find a gentle, sacred space.
With every breath, let worries cease,
In glimmering tranquility, find peace.

Moonlit Blankets of White

In the quiet of the night,
A blanket spread so white.
Whispers of the moonlight,
Casting dreams in soft sight.

Snowflakes dance in a swirl,
Nature's beauty in a twirl.
Each flake tells a story,
Of winter's calm, its glory.

Trees wear coats of silver lace,
In this serene, tranquil space.
Footprints tell of lovers' tread,
In the hush where few have led.

Stars above shimmer bright,
Guiding wanderers in flight.
Peaceful hearts find their way,
Underneath the moon's array.

Silent moments softly greet,
With every breath, hearts beat.
Wrapped in warmth from the chill,
In the night, the world stands still.

Echoes of a Frosted World

In the forest, silence reigns,
Frosty air, it softly pains.
Echoes of a world asleep,
In the cold, the secrets keep.

Branches crack in the calm,
Nature's chilly, soothing balm.
Whispers carried on the breeze,
Through the pines, past frozen trees.

Hoarfrost gleams on every edge,
Making paths a crystal hedge.
Footsteps crunch, a fleeting sound,
In this wonderland, I'm bound.

Winter's breath, a gentle sigh,
Underneath the endless sky.
Echoes linger, faint and clear,
In this frosted atmosphere.

Time stands still, forever slow,
In the white, soft waves of snow.
Each step forward, nature's art,
Echoes sing within my heart.

Glistening Secrets of the Night

Beneath the veil of starlit skies,
Secrets glisten, hidden ties.
In the shadows, dreams take flight,
Whispers caught in the night.

Dewdrops cling to blades of grass,
Mirroring the moon's soft mass.
Every glimmer holds a tale,
Of the night where wishes sail.

In the dark, the world transforms,
Where silence, like a river, swarms.
Glistening paths lead us on,
Underneath the cosmic dawn.

Veils of mist, a gentle touch,
Hold the night's enchantment much.
Every breeze, a breath of fate,
Secrets linger, never late.

As the shadows softly fade,
And the dawn begins to shade,
Glistening dreams softly part,
Leaving echoes in the heart.

Reflecting the Silent Drift

In the twilight's gentle flow,
Softly falls the silent snow.
Blanketing the world in peace,
As the busy moments cease.

Mirrored lakes hold winter's face,
Reflecting all with quiet grace.
Ripples dance, a fleeting sight,
In the glow of fading light.

Every flake that tumbles down,
Cushions dreams on sleepy town.
Whispers wrapped in winter's breath,
In this silence, we find depth.

Branches bow under the weight,
Of the snow that won't abate.
Nature's pulse is slow and true,
In this canvas, white and blue.

As the world begins to drift,
In these moments, spirits lift.
Reflecting stillness, pure and bright,
In the beauty of the night.

Frosted Kaleidoscope

In the morning light, all aglow,
Colors swirl in winter's flow.
Nature paints an icy frame,
Each flake whispers a crystalline name.

Through the branches, diamonds gleam,
A patchwork quilt, a frozen dream.
Every turn, a shifting hue,
Magic drifts in skies of blue.

Winds of whisper, soft and clear,
Echoes dance, the heart draws near.
Fractals form in twilight's chill,
A canvas forged by nature's will.

Underfoot, the crunch confides,
Secrets held where silence hides.
In this maze of sparkling white,
Life's reflections take their flight.

As dusk descends, the colors fade,
In stillness, the beauty laid.
Yet in dark's embrace, it stays,
A frost-kissed world in endless praise.

The Glow of Ice

Softly glowing in the night,
Ice ignites with a gentle light.
Moonlit beams on crystal floors,
Unlock magic behind closed doors.

Each frozen breath, a shimmer wakes,
The world glistens, as winter breaks.
A serene dance in silver grace,
Nature's breath, a glowing trace.

Hushed echoes drift on chilly air,
Illuminated dreams everywhere.
Frosted branches weave and twine,
Every shadow plans a sign.

Candles flicker against the cold,
Tales of warmth in blue and gold.
The night wraps tight in winter's seam,
A fragile, glowing, frozen dream.

In this landscape, the heart is free,
Under the ice, a mystery.
As stars twinkle from high above,
The glow unfolds, a tapestry of love.

Silent Sparkle

Amidst the woods, a quiet song,
Whispers of winter, soft and long.
In each flake, a note of grace,
Silent sparkle fills the space.

Beneath the branches, a glimmer rests,
Nature's jewels, the earth's best quests.
In the hush, the magic thrives,
A dance of peace, where stillness drives.

Each breath of air, a crystal tune,
Reflecting warmth beneath the moon.
Footprints trace a delicate path,
Leading forth from winter's math.

In shadows deep, the sparkles play,
Carving peace in their gentle sway.
Moments captured, ephemeral art,
Awakened dreams from nature's heart.

As daylight wanes, the frost does glow,
A symphony in the twilight's flow.
Silent warmth in the cold winds' call,
In every sparkle, the earth's enthrall.

Enchanted Frostbite

From the twilight's icy breath,
Whispers echo, a dance with death.
In the chill, enchantments sprout,
Frostbite tales woven throughout.

A lace of crystals, delicate thread,
Creeping softly where dreams are led.
Magic calls in the frosty air,
A world adorned, beyond compare.

With each step, the stories bloom,
Hidden secrets in winter's loom.
Branches sigh under icy weights,
Spheres of wonder that nature creates.

The moonlight casts a silver sheen,
A theater stage where frost has been.
In every breath, a spell ignites,
Enchantments found in coldest nights.

As shadows gather, spirits rise,
Holding tight to the frost-kissed skies.
Underneath the winter's bite,
Magic lingers, glowing bright.

Frost's Gentle Caress

In the hush of winter's breath,
A touch so soft and light,
Drifting crystals dance,
Shimmers in the night.

Veils of white enfold the ground,
Whispering a quiet song,
Nature's silence wraps around,
In this peace, we belong.

Branches wear their icy crown,
Glistening like precious stone,
Each sigh and shiver down,
This chill is not alone.

Underneath the pale moonlight,
Footsteps crunch like delicate glass,
Every shadow takes its flight,
Time slows as we pass.

Frost's embrace, so tender, sweet,
Enlightens the darkest night,
With every heartbeat, we greet,
This season's soft delight.

Whispers of the Crystal Night

Stars sprinkle the darkened sky,
Each twinkle tells a tale,
Of dreams that drift and sigh,
On a gentle, frosty trail.

A breath of winter in the air,
Awakens a world anew,
Every flake, a whispered care,
Miracles woven in the blue.

Moonlight kisses the sleeping trees,
Shadows dance with silent grace,
A melody that stirs the breeze,
In this tranquil, wondrous space.

All around, the stillness flows,
Carrying secrets, yearnings deep,
In the night, where magic grows,
In dreams, we softly leap.

Crystalline echoes fill the night,
A symphony of frosty dreams,
In every corner, pure delight,
Life unfolds in silver beams.

Mirror of the Arctic Sky

Above, the heavens stretch so wide,
Reflecting all that nature knows,
The Arctic sky, a breathtaking ride,
In shimmering light, the twilight glows.

Each star, a fragile, bright delight,
Kissing the vastness of the freeze,
In the hush of the frigid night,
Beauty whispers through the trees.

Deep blues and greens, a canvas rare,
Painted with dreams of icy breath,
Here, all burdens fade to air,
In this world of quiet death.

Auroras swirl, a dazzling dance,
Colors twine in cosmic play,
Invoking hope with every glance,
Transforming night to radiant day.

Through the mirror, we glimpse our fate,
In each reflection, warmth will rise,
Bound to love, we celebrate,
Underneath these Arctic skies.

Dreamy Frostflakes

In the cradle of the night,
Frostflakes fall like whispered dreams,
Delicate as soft moonlight,
Glinting in the silver streams.

Nature weaves its crystal art,
Each flake a story we can feel,
Painting love upon the heart,
In this rapture, we heal.

Twinkling softly in the air,
They dance like wishes, pure and bright,
Spreading joy beyond compare,
In this fleeting, fragile light.

Kissed by warmth of hopeful sighs,
Each drift a fleeting, tender kiss,
Frostflakes fall from starlit skies,
Leaving echoes of pure bliss.

As dawn breaks on the frosted ground,
Fading like a whispered song,
In the silence, peace is found,
In dreams, we still belong.

Twilit Snowflakes

In twilight's embrace, snowflakes fall,
Dancing gently, a silken thrall.
Whispered secrets, the cold wind brings,
Nature's magic, it softly sings.

Blankets white on the world so still,
Cradles dreams with a soft thrill.
Each flake unique, a story to share,
Glistening softly in frosty air.

Underneath the dusk's fading glow,
A wondrous blanket begins to grow.
The night's cool breath, a tender sigh,
As stars emerge in the velvet sky.

Footsteps muffled on the snowy floor,
Memories linger from days of yore.
With every flake, a wish takes flight,
In this gentle hush, all feels right.

So let the twilit snowflakes spin,
A tale of wonder, where dreams begin.
For in their dance, we find our way,
Through winter's charm, we long to stay.

Winter's Celestial Canvas

Upon the sky, a canvas bright,
Winter paints with purest white.
Stars like diamonds, twinkling high,
A masterpiece in the deep night sky.

Brush strokes bold, and shadows soft,
Each winter's tale aloft.
Nebulas drift, as the frozen night,
Wraps the earth in its silent flight.

Silhouettes of trees, in silver sheen,
A world transformed, serene and clean.
Echoes of laughter, in the crisp air,
Beauty surrounds, beyond compare.

In this moment, time stands still,
A quiet peace, a gentle thrill.
Nature's art, a wondrous sight,
Winter's canvas, pure delight.

Let your heart wander, your spirit soar,
In this realm of frost, forevermore.
Beneath the stars, we find our place,
In winter's grace, a warm embrace.

Icy Tranquility

In icy realms of hush and peace,
Where winter's whispers never cease.
Crystal waters mirror the sky,
Reflecting dreams as moments fly.

Silence holds a sacred space,
In frozen beauty, we find grace.
Gentle flakes drift, then alight,
Painting landscapes pure and white.

Branches bow with a crystal crown,
Nature's jewels, escaping frown.
Beneath the layer of glistening frost,
A world renewed, no moment lost.

The chilly air, a thrilling balm,
In icy tranquility, we feel calm.
With every breath, we sense the art,
Of winter's magic that warms the heart.

So let us wander through this land,
Hand in hand, as fate had planned.
For within this tranquil, icy embrace,
We find our peace, our sacred space.

Luminescent Crystals

Underneath the moon's soft glow,
Luminescent crystals start to show.
Glistening bright in the midnight air,
A thousand gems, so rare, so fair.

Each facet catches the faintest light,
Dancing shadows, a breathtaking sight.
In the stillness, they twirl and gleam,
A winter's wonder, like a dream.

Frosty tendrils weave a tale,
In nature's art, we set our sail.
With every sparkle, a promise made,
In icy realms, our fears allayed.

The night is young and the air is crisp,
As we gather under the celestial lisp.
With hands outstretched, we catch the fall,
Of luminescent crystals, enchanting all.

In this embrace, we lose all care,
With winter's magic, a fleeting affair.
So let the night wrap us in its cloak,
And share with us the secrets it spoke.

Winter's Dreamscape

Softly falls the silent snow,
Whispers in the night do glow.
Blankets of white stretch far and wide,
In this dreamscape, hearts abide.

Moonlight dances on frosty trees,
Chilled embrace of winter's breeze.
Stars ignite the velvet sky,
In this stillness, spirits fly.

Footprints mark a path so dear,
Echoes of laughter linger near.
Every breath a cloud of white,
Woven dreams in purest light.

Icicles hang like crystal tears,
Whispering tales from frozen years.
Nature sleeps wrapped in delight,
Cradled softly by the night.

In this world of ice and snow,
A tranquil peace begins to grow.
Winter's heart beats loud and strong,
In this dreamscape, we belong.

Tranquil Glimmer

A glimmer shines upon the ground,
Winter's kiss softly renowned.
Frosty patterns etched with grace,
Nature's art in calm embrace.

Whispers carried on the air,
Fragrant pine, and cedar bare.
Silent woods with secrets old,
Stories of the brave unfold.

Moonbeams weave through branches thin,
Silver lace where dreams begin.
Each step crunch beneath my feet,
A tranquil path, so pure, so sweet.

Stars twinkle in the endless night,
Guiding lost souls toward the light.
A journey in the frozen glow,
Through tranquil glimmers, spirits flow.

Embrace the stillness, let it stay,
Winter's beauty leads the way.
In every breath, a world anew,
In tranquil glimmer, hope shines through.

Radiant Snowflakes

Snowflakes dance on winter's breath,
Gentle whispers, life from death.
Each flake unique, a work of art,
Falling softly, they play their part.

Like diamonds scattered, pure and bright,
Glistening under gentle light.
Every landing, a fleeting grace,
In the quiet, find your place.

Children laugh as snowballs fly,
Joyful shouts beneath the sky.
Warmth of hearts in icy play,
Radiant moments light the day.

Crisp air tinged with magic thrill,
Nature whispers, calm and still.
In this wonder, feel alive,
In radiant snowflakes, love will thrive.

As the sun begins to rise,
Colors burst in brilliant skies.
These fleeting gems we hold so dear,
Radiant snowflakes, bring us cheer.

Serene Winter's Touch

Winter drapes a soft embrace,
Gentle touch upon the face.
Nature sleeps in blankets deep,
In serene moments, memories keep.

Flickering flames in hearths aglow,
Warmth within as cold winds blow.
Sipping cocoa, laughter rings,
In the heart, the winter sings.

Branches bow, laden with snow,
Each flake holds a tale to show.
The world wrapped in tranquil peace,
In winter's touch, all worries cease.

Footfalls soft on snowy trails,
Carried high on winter gales.
With every step, a world reborn,
In serene touch, lost hearts are worn.

As twilight descends, stars ignite,
Gentle whispers, a lullaby's light.
In this haven, love and such,
We find peace in winter's touch.

Frozen Fairytale

In whispers soft, the snowflakes fall,
A blanket white, embracing all.
The trees adorned in crystal light,
A tranquil scene, a dream in sight.

The lanterns glow, a warm embrace,
As shadows dance in winter's grace.
Footprints lead to a world serene,
In frozen fairytales, we dream.

The frost-kissed air, a playful tease,
Nature rests with gentle ease.
A time for peace, a moment's rest,
In winter's arms, we feel our best.

With laughter echoing through the night,
Children play in pure delight.
Each twirl and spin in snowbound glee,
A magical dance, wild and free.

So let us bask in this delight,
As stars twinkle in the night.
For here in frozen fairytale land,
We hold the wonders, hand in hand.

Luminescent Winter's Breath

Underneath a velvet sky,
The world aglow, a magic high.
With icy breath, the night awakes,
A shimmer soft, as morning breaks.

The moonlight bathes the trees in white,
As secrets whisper with the night.
Each branch adorned in crystal beads,
A tapestry from winter's seeds.

Through frosted panes, the light does dance,
Inviting dreams in sweet romance.
A hush descends, the air so pure,
In winter's breath, we find the cure.

The stars above, a guiding thread,
As twilight falls, we leave our bed.
In this embrace, we come alive,
In frozen realms, our spirits thrive.

So let us wander 'neath the moon,
With hearts aglow, we'll find our tune.
For in this world, so bright and clear,
We breathe the magic, free from fear.

Woven in Ice

A tapestry of glistening frost,
In nature's art, we count the cost.
Each crystal formed with tender care,
Woven in ice, a wonder rare.

Beneath the canopy of stars,
The world feels calm, despite the scars.
With every step, a crackle sound,
In this still night, our hearts are found.

The winter winds, they sing their song,
Of days gone by and nights so long.
A melody of dreams set free,
Woven in ice, our harmony.

Through bitter cold and silent night,
Our hopes unfold, a spark of light.
For in this chill, we find our way,
In dreams and whispers, we shall stay.

So take my hand beneath the sky,
For what is lost we'll learn to fly.
In every breath, a story grows,
Woven in ice, our love will glow.

Sparkling Hush of Twilight

In twilight's hush, the world does gleam,
With colors soft that softly dream.
A sparkling hush surrounds the night,
As stars awaken, shining bright.

The shadows stretch, the cold draws near,
Yet warmth breaks through, dispelling fear.
As nature whispers, stories old,
In twilight's embrace, magic unfolds.

The snowflakes fall like wishes sent,
Each drift a moment, time well spent.
In every corner, wonders lie,
Beneath the blanket, dreams will fly.

As frosty breath paints windows white,
We gather close to share the light.
In conversations soft and slow,
Within this hush, our love will grow.

So let the twilight wrap us tight,
In sparkling hues of deep twilight.
For here in stillness, hearts align,
In sparkling hush, your hand in mine.

Prism of Winter

In the crisp air, colors gleam,
Winter's breath whispers a dream.
Icicles hang like crystal lace,
Nature's canvas, a frozen embrace.

Branches spark with a silvery light,
Twinkling stars in the depth of night.
Snowflakes twirl in a dance so bright,
Capturing moments, pure and white.

Footprints trace through fields of frost,
Paths of silence, where time seems lost.
Each step echoes in the quiet glow,
A world transformed by the falling snow.

Underneath the vast, endless sky,
The winter's beauty makes hearts sigh.
Every flake a story, softly spun,
In the prism of winter, we become one.

Night descends, the horizon glows,
The warmth of candlelight softly flows.
In this stillness, peace takes flight,
As dreams unfold in the shimmering night.

Light-Frosted Tranquility

Gentle flakes drift from the sky,
A soft whisper, winter's sigh.
Each breath a cloud in the chilled air,
Wraps the world in a quiet prayer.

Trees adorned in crystal white,
Glistening softly in the moonlight.
Silhouettes dance on the frosty ground,
Tranquility in silence profound.

Frozen lakes mirror the stars,
Nature's jewels, no bounds or bars.
In this stillness, hearts align,
Finding solace in the divine.

Snow-covered hills, a gentle sweep,
Secrets held in the drifts so deep.
Time slows down, the world takes pause,
In this moment, we reflect cause.

Evening whispers a tranquil hymn,
Light-frosted dreams where visions brim.
Wrapped in warmth, our spirits flow,
Finding peace in the winter's glow.

Winter's Hidden Glow

Beneath the blanket of purest white,
Lies a warmth that hides from sight.
In frozen fields, a glow resides,
A gentle magic in winter's tides.

Shadows cast by the waning sun,
Silent beauty, a race just run.
Softly creeping through the dark,
Winter's charm ignites a spark.

The night reveals a twinkling trance,
Stars reflect on the snow's expanse.
Each breath inhaled whispers delight,
In every corner, a secret light.

Frosted windows frame the scene,
A world alive, serene and keen.
In the hush, a story unfolds,
Of hidden treasures that winter holds.

As dawn breaks, a canvas bright,
Reveals the wonders of the night.
In the heart of winter, we find our glow,
A reminder that warmth can always flow.

Luminous Drift

Snowflakes glisten, a soft cascade,
Each one a whisper, each one a trade.
Carpeted paths where shadows play,
In the luminous drift of the day.

Moonlight dances on the frozen streams,
Reflecting secrets and silent dreams.
Quiet echoes of forgotten lore,
Softly beckoning us to explore.

Whispers of nature in the still air,
A touch of frost, delicate and rare.
Each flake a wonder, each flake a gift,
In the beauty of winter's gentle drift.

Branches bow under the weight of snow,
Nature's artwork in a pure tableau.
Moments captured in transient grace,
In every drift, there's a warm embrace.

As twilight deepens, stars emerge,
Winter's beauty begins to surge.
Among the drifts, hope takes flight,
In luminous magic, we find our light.

Glinting Evening Stillness

The sun sinks low in the sky,
Painting hues of orange and gray.
A quiet hush wraps the land,
As night whispers soft, drifting away.

Stars begin their gentle dance,
Glinting bright in the vast abyss.
Moonlight spills on silver streams,
A serenade of celestial bliss.

Trees stand tall, their shadows stretch,
Casting dreams upon the ground.
In the stillness, hearts find peace,
In this evening, calm and profound.

The world wears a cloak of night,
With secrets softly tucked away.
In the glinting evening's grace,
Hope and wonder come out to play.

Breeze whispers tales of old,
As it sweeps through leaves and eaves.
Every sigh and breath resounds,
In the stillness, the heart believes.

Frosty Wishes

In the quiet chill of dawn,
Frosty wishes drift like dreams.
Each breath a cloud that dances,
In this wonderland of gleams.

Branches dressed in crystal lace,
Sparkling under morning's light.
Whispers of hope in the air,
As the day begins its flight.

Snowflakes twirl on gentle breezes,
Each a wish from skies above.
Nature's gift, a soft embrace,
Wrapped in winter's tender love.

Children laugh with rosy cheeks,
Building castles, pure delight.
Frosty wishes shared in joy,
Under the glow of soft twilight.

As evening falls, the world is still,
A blanket white, calm and bright.
Frosty wishes softly linger,
In the magic of the night.

Radiant Slumber

Nestled in the arms of night,
A tranquil hush blankets the earth.
Stars twinkle softly, a glowing sight,
Welcoming dreams, bringing mirth.

Moonbeams weave through window panes,
A tender glow, a gentle guide.
In radiant slumber, the heart remains,
While the world outside silently glides.

Whispers of dreams begin to play,
In the silence, hopes unite.
Floating on clouds of soft decay,
In the depths of soothing night.

The calm of dusk cradles all,
Wrapped in stillness, soft and warm.
Radiant slumber's sweet enthrall,
Cocooned in peace, safe from harm.

Morning will come with a gentle touch,
Awakening souls from their rest.
But for now, in dreams we clutch,
In radiant slumber, life is blessed.

Hushed Snowflakes Fall

In the twilight, whispers blend,
Hushed snowflakes softly glide.
Each flake a tale, a gentle friend,
Spreading peace across the wide.

Blanketing roofs and winding lanes,
A quiet world, untouched and free.
Nature hums soft, like gentle rains,
As snowflakes fall, a symphony.

Children twirl in joy and glee,
Creating memories etched in white.
Every flake, a mystery,
Dancing in the softening light.

The world holds its breath in awe,
As beauty takes its rightful stand.
Hushed snowflakes write their laws,
In silence, a new day is planned.

As night drapes her velvet cloak,
Stars emerge to see the scene.
In a wonderland where dreams invoke,
Hushed snowflakes fall, pure and serene.

Ethereal Chill

A whisper of frost in the night,
Silvery stars take their flight.
Trees sway with a gentle grace,
Nature's breath, a cold embrace.

Crystal skies, so deep and vast,
Dreams float softly, unsurpassed.
Echoes of silence fill the air,
In this world, we find our share.

The moon casts shadows, serene and bright,
A dance of shadows in the light.
Time stands still, in a gentle thrill,
Heartbeats soft, in the winter chill.

Hushed whispers stir the silent space,
With every breath, we find our place.
Wrapped in the arms of the cold night's sway,
We linger here, till break of day.

A Soft White Blanket

A soft white blanket on the ground,
Whispers of snow without a sound.
Nature's quilt, a gentle sigh,
Frosty patterns that dance and fly.

Each flake unique, a fleeting kiss,
In winter's hold, we find our bliss.
Footprints linger, a tale to tell,
In this peaceful world, all is well.

Branches bow beneath the weight,
The tranquil stillness, a wondrous state.
The chill wraps close, like a warm embrace,
In the soft white blanket, we find our place.

Sunrise glimmers, the frost will fade,
Yet in our hearts, the memories stayed.
A fleeting moment, so pure, so bright,
In the still of winter's gentle night.

Radiant Shadows

In the dusk, where light meets night,
Shadows stretch, an artful sight.
Figures dance in twilight's glow,
Mysteries in the dark, we know.

With each step, a story unfolds,
The warmth of the sun, as daylight scolds.
Silhouettes sway under branches bare,
Whispers of secrets float in the air.

Radiant hues paint the fading sky,
Golden moments as day bids goodbye.
Nighttime's curtain falls with grace,
Embracing the world in a soft embrace.

In this magic, we lose our fear,
For shadows are friends who draw us near.
So let us wander through this ballet,
Where daylight meets night, in radiant display.

Moonlit Drifts

The moonlight glimmers on the lake,
Silver trails in every wake.
Soft whispers of night take flight,
Guiding dreams in pale moonlight.

Gentle waves that kiss the shore,
Crickets sing, a sweet encore.
Across the water, shadows play,
While stars above hold sway.

In the stillness, hearts unwind,
Every secret of the mind.
Wrapped in wonder, we drift away,
Chasing visions until the day.

The world is paused; time's a friend,
In this place, where worries end.
Beneath the light of the golden sphere,
We find our peace, our hopes draw near.

With each breath, the night unfolds,
Stories written in starlit gold.
In moonlit drifts, we come alive,
In dreams so sweet, our spirits thrive.

Winter's Veil

Snowflakes fall from the sky,
Blanketing the earth below.
Trees wear robes of purest white,
In the hush of winter's glow.

Frosty breath hangs in the air,
Whispers dance on icy streets.
Footsteps crunch on frozen ground,
Nature's heart skips joyful beats.

Candles flicker in the night,
Casting shadows, soft and warm.
By the fire, we gather close,
Safe and sound from winter's storm.

Stars emerge in velvet skies,
Winking down from heights untold.
Winter's magic fills our hearts,
A timeless tale, forever bold.

As the world rests and renews,
Dreams take flight on chilly breeze.
Hope is wrapped in winter's veil,
Whispered softly through the trees.

Sparkling Chill

Morning light breaks on the snow,
Sparkling jewels in the dawn.
Nature shimmers, pure and bright,
A tranquil world, peaceful, drawn.

Gentle winds caress the pines,
A symphony of crisp delight.
Whispers of a winter song,
Carry through the tranquil night.

Icicles hang like chandeliers,
Glistening in the pale sunlight.
Each breath forms a cloud of dreams,
As day unfolds, a pure insight.

Footprints leading through the glades,
Mark the path of wanderers bold.
In this world of sparkling chill,
Stories of winter yet unfold.

As twilight wraps the day in hues,
We gather 'round the fireside cheer.
With warmth and laughter shared anew,
We celebrate this time of year.

Moonlit Silence

Silver beams on quiet night,
Bathed in the moon's soft glow.
Stars shimmer in the vast expanse,
Guiding dreams where lovers go.

Whispers travel on the breeze,
Secrets held by night's embrace.
Every shadow tells a tale,
In this calm and sacred space.

Frost adorns each tree and stone,
Nature holds its breath in awe.
Underneath the silver light,
We find magic in the raw.

Footsteps soften on the ground,
Gentle echoes, soft and clear.
In the moonlit silence found,
Hearts unite without a fear.

As the night unfolds its charm,
We find peace in twilight's grace.
Together in this quiet hour,
We cherish time and sacred space.

Icy Splendor

Crystal streams flow over stones,
Mirror images of the sky.
Mountains dressed in white embrace,
The beauty where the eagles fly.

Branches heavy, bowed in grace,
Nature's art, a masterpiece.
In the stillness, we can feel,
A world transformed, a sweet release.

Shadows dance on frozen lakes,
Framed by trees with frosty crowns.
Every corner holds a spark,
Nature's joy wears winter's gowns.

In this realm of icy splendor,
Our souls awaken, breathe anew.
Carving paths through snow and chill,
Each moment whispers, 'start anew.'

As seasons shift and fade from sight,
We hold these memories dear.
In every flake and twinkling star,
Lives a magic that draws us near.

Frozen Lullaby

Silent night, the world does sleep,
In blankets soft, the dreams we keep.
Whispers low, in shadows glide,
Snowflakes dance, a gentle tide.

Moonlight casts a silver glow,
Through frosted trees, the cold winds blow.
Stars above, they watch and sigh,
Embraced in peace, no need for why.

A quiet heart, a tranquil song,
In winter's arms, we all belong.
With each breath, a chilly mist,
In this calm, we find our bliss.

Dreamers dream, and lovers sigh,
Underneath the starlit sky.
Whispers soft, and fingers trace,
A frozen world, a shared embrace.

Wrapped in warmth, the fire glows,
Outside wraps a chill, it shows.
In cozy nooks, our stories spun,
This frozen lullaby, we've won.

Winter's Embrace

In the woods where silence reigns,
Beneath the weight of gentle chains.
Nature dons her crystal dress,
With each flake, she shows her finesse.

Branches bowed with heavy snow,
Laughter hides where cold winds blow.
Wrapped in warmth, we share a tale,
Of winter's strength and fragile veil.

The sun sets low, a golden sphere,
Casting shadows, sharp and clear.
We gather close, our hearts aglow,
In winter's arms, we learn to grow.

Soft whispers of the frosty air,
Glistening paths where few may dare.
Hand in hand, we stroll the night,
In winter's embrace, all feels right.

As the skies begin to gray,
We find warmth in the fading day.
In every breath, a chill remains,
Yet love ignites, as hope sustains.

Illuminated Frost

Dawn breaks slowly, the world unveiled,
Frosty jewels where cold winds hailed.
Sunlight dances on icy lakes,
Nature's canvas, beauty wakes.

Glistening threads in morning light,
Transforming earth with pure delight.
Every step, a crunching sound,
A tapestry of joy surrounds.

Shadows play on glistening ground,
As silence wraps the world around.
With every breath, we breathe in grace,
Illuminated, this sacred space.

Through sparkling trees, the sunlight streams,
We wander deeper, lost in dreams.
With every moment, magic grows,
In the heart, a warmth that glows.

As twilight falls, the chill descends,
But still the light within us blends.
With frosted breath, we softly sing,
Illuminated frost, the joy you bring.

Shimmering Thaw

Winter melts to spring's embrace,
Gentle whispers, a softer pace.
Drips of water, sweet refrain,
Echoes of the lost refrain.

Bare branches reach for skies anew,
As softest blooms begin to strew.
Colors burst where white once lay,
Promising a bright new day.

In the thaw, the world awakes,
Life unleashed, the earth remakes.
Every whisper of the breeze,
Carries scents that tease and please.

Sunshine pools on the forest floor,
Kissing ice to be no more.
Frolicking in radiant beams,
Nature dances, wakes from dreams.

In every drop, a story flows,
Of shimmering thaw, where love grows.
With open hearts, we greet the morn,
In the light of spring, we're reborn.

Crystal Dreams

In the night, they shimmer bright,
Whispers soft in silver light.
Dancing shadows, secrets shared,
In the stillness, hearts laid bare.

Woven tales of fragile gleam,
Lost in the fabric of a dream.
Every glance, a wish held tight,
Starlit echoes fill the night.

Glistening paths where wishes soar,
On crystal wings, we search for more.
With every breath, a spark ignites,
In the glow of endless nights.

Beneath the moon, we chase the gleam,
In this world, we dare to dream.
Together, lost in time's embrace,
Carried forth in velvet space.

And as dawn breaks the spell we weave,
In crystal dreams, we learn to believe.
Hand in hand, we rise anew,
In a realm where love shines through.

Frosted Serenade

A gentle hush upon the trees,
Whispers float upon the breeze.
Snowflakes fall, a soft ballet,
In winter's heart, we drift away.

Chilled reflections, icy sights,
Dancing under silver lights.
Every note a winter's song,
In this world, we both belong.

Voices echo, soft and clear,
Carried forth by frosty air.
Melodies of purest white,
Harmonies beneath the night.

As stars twinkle in frozen skies,
We find warmth in each other's eyes.
Frosted dreams, a perfect rhyme,
In this moment, space and time.

With every breath, a crystal tune,
Underneath the watchful moon.
Together, lost in winter's balm,
In a frosted, tranquil calm.

Silver Veil

In twilight's hush, a silver veil,
Wrapped in whispers, soft and frail.
Veiled secrets of the closing day,
In shadows lost, we softly sway.

Glisten faintly, stars appear,
Nights unfold, serene and clear.
Underneath the silver glow,
Hearts awaken, gently flow.

Dreams entwined in twilight's calm,
Lifting spirits like a psalm.
Every sigh, a breath of grace,
In this sacred, timeless place.

As night drapes stars overhead,
In quiet moments, words unsaid.
With every heartbeat, silence grows,
In a world where stillness flows.

Beneath this veil, we find our song,
In the night where we belong.
Hand in hand, our spirits rise,
In the dancing silver skies.

Chilling Radiance

In the stillness, cold winds play,
Radiance shines at close of day.
Chilling breaths of winter's grace,
In frosted air, we find our place.

Glimmers dance on frozen streams,
In the silence, scattered dreams.
Every touch, a cooling flame,
In this radiance, we find names.

Moonlight bathes the world in gold,
Whispered tales of love retold.
Through the chill, our hearts ignite,
Warmth discovered in the night.

With every heartbeat, time stands still,
Chilling radiance, hearts to fill.
Underneath the stars' embrace,
In the stillness, find our place.

Together bound in frosty glow,
Where every feeling starts to flow.
In this radiant, chilling spree,
Our souls entwined, forever free.

Velvet White Silence

Snowflakes drift in gentle grace,
A blanket lies on the world's embrace.
Whispers soft, a soothing sound,
In this quiet, peace is found.

Trees wear coats of purest white,
The stars above twinkle bright.
Night wraps all in tender care,
Sweet silence fills the still, cold air.

Footsteps crunch on frosty ground,
Echoes fade without a sound.
Moonlit paths weave through the night,
In velvet warmth, the heart takes flight.

Pine trees sway, a soft ballet,
Guided by the wind's soft play.
Glimmers dance on snowflakes bright,
Nature's beauty in soft light.

With every breath, a frosty cloud,
The world is hushed, the sky is proud.
In this moment, time stands still,
Wrapped in dreams, we gently chill.

Moonbeams on Ice

Silver light on frozen lake,
Shimmers where the shadows break.
Ice so clear, a mirror bright,
Reflecting all the stars at night.

Gentle whispers in the breeze,
Rustling through the barren trees.
Moonbeams dance, a wild trace,
As nature finds its quiet grace.

In the stillness, spirits roam,
Warming hearts, far from home.
Each glimmer tells a tale so old,
Of secrets in the night, retold.

Frosty breath hangs in the air,
Magic fills this world so fair.
Steps taken in a soft embrace,
Finding joy in winter's face.

Laughter echoes on the ice,
Friendship forms in this paradise.
In moonlight's glow, together we glide,
With hearts so warm, and spirits wide.

Shining Veils of Winter

Morning breaks with a silver hue,
Veils of frost in shades of blue.
Nature drapes in shimmering light,
A radiant, breathtaking sight.

Crystal flakes fall soft and slow,
Covering the world below.
Each branch, each leaf, adorned with care,
Winter's kiss, a season rare.

Fields of white stretch far and near,
Whispers of the cold draw near.
Cotton clouds in skies of grey,
Wrap the earth in soft array.

Children play in playful dives,
Joyful echoes richly thrive.
Sleds and laughter fill the air,
In this wonderland so rare.

As twilight falls, a warming glow,
Stars appear in velvet show.
Veils of winter gently weave,
In dreams that we believe.

A Tapestry of Frost

Frosty fingers touch the panes,
Crafting art in crystal chains.
Nature's brush in cold creates,
A tapestry that time awaits.

Each pattern tells of winter's lore,
Whispers of the days before.
Delicate lace, in light it glows,
A timeless beauty, nature shows.

Underneath the starry dome,
Winter sings a chilling poem.
Branches bare, yet full of grace,
Every curve a warm embrace.

Footprints lead through fields of white,
Tracing dreams in moonlight bright.
Laughter mingles with the breeze,
Echoing through the frozen trees.

As day departs, the twilight sings,
Wings of night on gentle springs.
In the dark, the world finds peace,
A tapestry where wonders cease.

Threads of the Winter Light

In the hush of twilight's glow,
Softly falls the shimmering snow.
Threads of silver weave the scene,
Painting earth in a dream-like sheen.

Bare branches stretch to the sky,
Where whispered secrets linger nigh.
Glowing softly, the light retreats,
As dusk wraps around the frostbit streets.

Echoes dance in the crisp night air,
Glimmers of magic everywhere.
With each breath, a pause ensues,
Winter's breath brings with it clues.

Stars awaken, twinkling bright,
Guiding our hearts in the quiet night.
Threads of warmth in the bitter cold,
Stories of love and life unfold.

Time slows down in this winter's grace,
Nature's beauty, a soft embrace.
Each moment cherished, pure delight,
In the glow of threads of winter light.

Luminous Whispers of Ice

Through the clarity of icy breath,
Luminous whispers dance with death.
Glints of crystal, pure and rare,
Adorn the world with a tender care.

Echoes shimmer in the chill,
Promising peace, a longing will.
Every flake a story told,
In the softness of winter's fold.

Footsteps crunch on frozen ground,
Silent moments, beauty found.
Moonlight weaves through the trees,
A gentle voice carried by the breeze.

As shadows lengthen, spirits rise,
In this realm, the heart complies.
Luminous whispers float on high,
Binding us to the vast, dark sky.

Each heartbeat echoes, soft and slow,
In the tapestry of winter's glow.
A promise held in icy grace,
Luminous whispers, time's embrace.

Frosted Horizons

Beyond the hills where shadows meet,
Frosted horizons, a quiet feat.
Nature wears a sparkling crown,
Beneath the weight of a snowy gown.

Sunrise kisses the icy crust,
A golden glow, a gentle gust.
Whispers of hope in the bitter air,
Frosted horizons beyond compare.

Fields of white, a canvas bright,
Each step forward, a dance of light.
Carefree moments in winter's breath,
Chasing warmth that conquers death.

Through the stillness, a soft refrain,
The heart beats steady, free from pain.
Frosted horizons speak of peace,
In winter's beauty, hearts find release.

Beneath the surface, life awaits,
In every flake, hope resonates.
Frosted horizons call us near,
A tranquil promise, ever clear.

Winter's Whisper

In the echo of silence, soft and deep,
Winter's whisper beckons, secrets to keep.
Crisp and clear, the air so light,
Embracing all in a shrouded night.

The moon hangs low, a watchful eye,
Casting shadows that quietly sigh.
Beneath the surface, stories unfold,
Of winter's magic, timeless and bold.

Frosted leaves glisten in twilight's gown,
Nature whispers as daylight drowns.
Each flake a promise, each breeze a song,
In the stillness, we all belong.

Gathered close by the fire's warm glow,
Hearts entwined in the winter's flow.
Winter's whisper calls us near,
In every silence, love draws near.

As the world cradles the night sky's hue,
Winter's whisper paints it anew.
In every breath, a quiet grace,
Winter's secret, a warm embrace.

Icy Harmony

In silence pure, the frost does gleam,
Whispers of winter, a gentle dream.
Branches cloaked in shimmering white,
Nature's music in the still of night.

Stars above in the deep-blue sky,
Glistening tears as they float on by.
A dance of shadows, a ballet of light,
Harmony crafted in the soft twilight.

Footsteps crunch on a blanket of snow,
Each sound a secret, a tale to bestow.
Breath visible, in the crisp, cool air,
The world wrapped in warmth of tender care.

Moonlight kisses the frozen stream,
Reflecting dreams, a radiant beam.
Bridges of ice span the winter's breath,
Uniting life, defeating death.

So let us wander through this glade,
In the icy magic that won't soon fade.
Hearts entwined in a tranquil embrace,
Finding beauty in the cold's quiet grace.

Shifting White Mirage

A canvas vast, painted in white,
Mirages dance in the soft twilight.
Footprints vanish, swallowed by snow,
Ghostly echoes of where we go.

Horizons blur in the shifting light,
Illusions flicker, then take flight.
Whispers of frost, in the chilly air,
A fleeting glimpse of what we dare.

Glistening crystals in a crystal dome,
Nature's artistry, a wintry home.
Shadows stretch like fingers long,
In the cold realm, we hum our song.

The chill embraces, a tender kiss,
In the abyss, we find our bliss.
Dreams conjured in the swirling haze,
Lost in the magic of winter's ways.

Majesty rests on each frosted leaf,
In silence, we find the heart's relief.
Through shifting visions, we forge ahead,
In this mirage, we leave our dread.

Celestial Chill

Stars ignite in a velvet sky,
A blanket of chill, where dreams can fly.
Cosmic whispers on winter's breath,
Illuminating life in the dance of death.

In the stillness, galaxies swirl,
In the heart of night, our thoughts unfurl.
Amidst the glow of a shivering moon,
Awakened wishes, softly croon.

Celestial bodies in their embrace,
Crafting stories in the emptiness of space.
Frosted pathways lead to the bright,
Footsteps tracing paths of starlight.

A chill that lingers, a breath so light,
Embracing the wonder, igniting the night.
Hearts alight with the spark of hope,
In the cosmic sea, together we cope.

Through icy whispers, cosmos speaks,
In dreams of endless, we find the peaks.
Celestial wonders, a chilling thrill,
In the vast expanse, our hearts stand still.

Resplendent Ice

Behold the splendor, the glistening glass,
Where the world reflects as seasons pass.
Icicles hang like nature's light,
Resplendent ice, a striking sight.

Crystal shards that shimmer and shine,
Nature's brilliance creates the divine.
Frozen rivers in a quiet dance,
Inviting souls to take a chance.

Underneath the winter's cloak,
Whispers echo in every stroke.
Each breath of frost a story to tell,
In the silence where the heart does dwell.

A canvas of dreams beneath the frost,
In the brilliance of ice, we find the lost.
Barriers break in the cold embrace,
Finding warmth in love's gentle trace.

Resplendent moments linger in air,
Painting life with colors rare.
Embrace the chill, let worries cease,
In the realm of ice, discover peace.

Frostbitten Echoes

In shadows deep, the silence reigns,
Whispers lost in winter's chains.
Footsteps muffled, soft and slow,
Echoes linger, where cold winds blow.

Icicles hang like memories past,
Each breath held tight, a moment cast.
Underneath the pale moonlight,
Frostbitten dreams take silent flight.

The world adorned in crystal white,
Nature sleeps in the stillness of night.
A world reborn, yet held at bay,
Frostbitten echoes fade away.

Through barren branches, shadows play,
A haunting dance of decay.
Time stands still, yet moves along,
In the chill, we find our song.

Winds will shift, and spring will call,
Transforming ice to life for all.
But in this moment, cold and clear,
Frostbitten echoes linger near.

Radiance of the Dawn

Awakening earth in colors bright,
Kissed by warmth of morning light.
Awash in hues of golden grace,
The day emerges, a soft embrace.

Birds take flight in the painted sky,
Songs of joy as shadows fly.
Dewdrops glisten on blades of grass,
A fleeting moment, here, then past.

Clouds stretch wide, a canvas new,
Brushing skies in every hue.
Hope is born where darkness laid,
A promise kept, a debt repaid.

As time unfurls, the sun ascends,
Life awakens, as daylight mends.
Radiance spreads, dispelling fears,
A symphony played through the years.

In every heart, a spark ignites,
Chasing shadows, finding light.
With every dawn, a tale unfolds,
Of journeys taken, of dreams retold.

Dimensional Frost

Layers of ice weave a tale,
Of worlds unseen, where shadows pale.
In every crystal, secrets lie,
Echoes of time, in silence, cry.

Textures shift, realities bend,
In frost's embrace, the edges blend.
A chill that cuts through heart and soul,
Where dimensions meet, we lose control.

Frosted breath in the wintry air,
Moments caught in a frozen stare.
Time retracts, and space distorts,
In this realm where nothing resorts.

Yet through the frost, a glimpse of light,
Pierces through the endless night.
Revealing paths, yet to be walked,
In the ethereal, we are talked.

Embrace the chill, let go of fear,
As dimensional frost draws near.
In the stillness, magic waits,
To guide us through the woven fates.

Chilly Haven

In the heart of winter's breath,
Lies a haven, kissed by death.
Snowflakes dance on whispered breeze,
A tranquil place where nature frees.

Glistening white on branches tall,
The world wrapped in a glistening shawl.
Silence reigns, a soothing balm,
In chilly haven, all is calm.

Evergreens hold secrets tight,
Guardians of the frosty night.
Beneath their shade, warm souls will tread,
In nature's arms, no more dread.

Crisp air bites, yet sparks delight,
As candles flicker in soft twilight.
Gathered close, we share our dreams,
Amidst the chill, warmth redeems.

With laughter echoing through the trees,
In chilly haven, we find ease.
A refuge from the world's harsh scorn,
In frozen beauty, love is born.

Glistening Wishes in the Air

Wishes float like paper planes,
Carried softly on the breeze.
Soft whispers dance in moonlit lanes,
Hoping hearts find sweet release.

Stars adorn the velvet night,
Each a dream that dares to soar.
Glistening hopes take gentle flight,
Yearning for forevermore.

In the silence, magic weaves,
A tapestry of whispered light.
Every thought that one believes,
Glows like fireflies in the night.

Beneath the sky's enchanting hue,
Promises shimmer, pure and bright.
With every sigh, intentions grew,
Finding peace in starry sight.

As dawn awakens, dreams may fade,
Yet wishes linger like a prayer.
In every heart, a spark displayed,
Glistening wishes in the air.

Crystal Illuminations

Crystals wake in morning light,
Shimmering in a silver glow.
Each facet catches dreams in flight,
A dance of shadows, ebb, and flow.

Softly, whispers of the dawn,
Guide the day with gentle arms.
In the quiet, hopes are drawn,
Embraced by nature's simple charms.

Winter's breath lays still and deep,
Frosted edges, pure and clear.
Every promise, secrets keep,
Sparkling thoughts that persevere.

Beneath the weight of snowy skies,
Life unfolds in graceful hush.
Crystal visions softly rise,
In the stillness, hearts can rush.

As daylight fades, reflections gleam,
Illuminated by the stars.
In crystal dreams, we find our theme,
Guided gently by our scars.

Nights Painted in White

Nights arrive, cloaked in white,
Blankets of quiet, soft and deep.
Moonlight dances, pure delight,
As the world slips into sleep.

Whispers ride on winter's breath,
Carried on a chill so bright.
In the silence, life finds its depth,
Stars twinkle, a wondrous sight.

Shadows stretch across the ground,
Echoes of a day long spent.
In this canvas, peace is found,
Nature's lullaby, heaven-sent.

Every flake, a fleeting dream,
Painting moments, rare and true.
Beneath the shimmer, hearts redeem,
For every night, a chance anew.

As dawn approaches, colors blend,
Melting softly into day.
Yet in memory, we will tend,
Nights painted white, forever stay.

Frosted Echoes

In the stillness, echoes ring,
Frosted whispers clothed in light.
Nature cradles everything,
In the arms of winter's night.

Every breath a cloud of dreams,
Each exhale a silent song.
Through the woods, the magic streams,
Where the echoes of hope belong.

Footsteps crunch on powdered earth,
With each step, memories bloom.
Frosted echoes bring rebirth,
Carrying warmth despite the gloom.

In the moments frozen tight,
We find solace, pure and rare.
In the dance of day to night,
Frosted echoes fill the air.

As we gather by the fire,
Stories weave through every heart.
Of frost and dreams that never tire,
Frosted echoes, a work of art.

Celestial Frost

In the stillness of night, soft whispers play,
Crystals shimmer where moonlight lay.
Each breath a cloud, a fleeting sigh,
Under the stars, the world drifts by.

Branches adorned in glittering lace,
Nature's beauty at a tranquil pace.
A blanket of white, pure as a dream,
Echoes of silence join in the gleam.

Glistening fields, a tranquil sight,
Frost-kissed memories in the soft twilight.
Every step crunches beneath the glow,
A dance with the night, in the frost we flow.

Whispers of winter, a soothing hymn,
Echoing gently, a world so dim.
Celestial wonders, a tapestry spun,
In the heart of cold, we are all one.

Time drifts slowly, wrapped in delight,
Frosty magic fills the night.
In this frozen embrace, we find our peace,
Celestial frost, a sweet release.

Enchanted Chill

Upon a breath, the chill enchants,
With every breeze, the heart it grants.
Frosted windows, patterns divine,
In this whisper, our souls entwine.

The twilight glows with bright silver lines,
As nature drinks in the starlit signs.
Each flake a wish, delicate and pure,
In the enchanted air, our dreams endure.

Winds carry secrets from ages past,
In the chill, memories hold fast.
Softly we wander through glades of white,
In the quiet of night, we take flight.

Echoes of laughter blend with the frost,
In this beauty, we never feel lost.
Under the arch of a starlit sky,
The enchanted chill makes spirits fly.

Each moment unfolds, like petals of snow,
In the embrace of winter, our hearts aglow.
Capturing magic in every still breath,
In this world of wonder, we conquer death.

Lighted Path through Frost

A lantern glows in the cold, crisp night,
Guiding me softly, a beacon of light.
Frosted whispers dance around my feet,
On this frozen path, where dreams meet.

Twinkling stars mirror the glow below,
Leading me onward through the soft, white snow.
Each step a promise, each breath a prayer,
In this frost-kissed world, free of all care.

The lighted path winds through the trees,
Carrying echoes of secrets with ease.
In the still of the night, a magic found,
In each soft shimmer, joy knows no bound.

Trail of silver leading to the unknown,
In this frosted realm, together we've grown.
With hope in our hearts, we dare to explore,
Through the lighted path, forevermore.

Unfolding wonders as shadows play,
In this serene moment, we drift away.
Lighting the way through winter's embrace,
In the beauty of frost, we find our place.

Chasing Icicle Shadows

Icicles hang like crystal spears,
Casting shadows fueled by fears.
The sun breaks through in playful tease,
Chasing whispers among the trees.

As shadows stretch on winter's breath,
They dance with lines that flirt with death.
Each one a story of silence and chill,
Fleeting moments, a heart to fill.

Fingers trace lines on frosted glass,
Glimmers of beauty, the seasons pass.
Chasing the light, as dreams unfold,
In the shadowed world, our tales are told.

With every step, we wander deeper,
Underneath, the heart grows steeper.
Icicle shadows whisper and sway,
In their embrace, we find our way.

A world transformed in the quiet glow,
Each flicker of light, a story to show.
Chasing shadows beneath the bright sun,
In this frost-kissed land, we become one.

Twinkling Tundra

Underneath the starry skies,
Snowflakes dance and softly rise.
Silent whispers, cool and bright,
Tundra glimmers in the night.

Frosty air, a gentle chill,
Echoes of the night so still.
Nights adorned with silver light,
Embracing all within their sight.

Footprints map the frozen ground,
In this world, pure joy is found.
Nature's canvas, wide and free,
A wondrous sight for all to see.

Chill of winter, crisp and clear,
Every heart feels calm and near.
Across the plains, the shadows play,
In twinkling dreams, we drift away.

In the stillness, echoes hum,
Nature's breath, a soft, sweet drum.
Every moment, held with grace,
In twinkling tundra's warm embrace.

Glacial Elegance

Icy crystals, sharp and bright,
Glistening in the pale moonlight.
Mountains draped in silver lace,
Whispering of nature's grace.

Each breath cool, a frosty sigh,
Underneath the vast, wide sky.
Rivers frozen, time stands still,
In the chill, we feel the thrill.

Glistening edges, sharp and fine,
Nature sculpted, pure design.
Winter's art, a silent sound,
In the splendor all around.

Softly falling, snowflakes twirl,
Floating down in perfect whirl.
Glacial beauty, calm and pure,
An elegance we all endure.

Beneath the surface, life abounds,
In icy realms where peace is found.
Winter's song, a hushed delight,
Glacial elegance ignites the night.

Whispering Flakes

Gentle drift of falling snow,
Whispers softly as they flow.
Each flake unique, a fleeting kiss,
In winter's realm, we find our bliss.

Twirling down from heavens high,
Painting landscapes, oh so shy.
Silent seasons come and go,
Whispering tales of frost and glow.

Fields aglow with blankets white,
Peaceful moments, pure delight.
In the hush, we pause and see,
Whispering flakes, they set us free.

Softly covering earth's embrace,
With each flake, we find our place.
A tapestry of purest dreams,
In winter's chill, heart gently beams.

Nature's breath, a quiet sigh,
Whispering softly, time slips by.
Cocooned in winter's snowy grace,
In the dance of flakes, we find our space.

The Light of Winter

Golden rays on snowy peaks,
Chasing shadows, warmth it seeks.
In the stillness, soft and bright,
The world awakens to the light.

Icicles glint with morning sun,
Whispers of the day begun.
Every corner shines anew,
In the glow, the heart breaks through.

Each breath steams in the crisp air,
Winter magic, everywhere.
Frosty branches, kissed with gold,
In the light, new stories told.

Fire flickers, ember's dance,
Cozy evenings, warm romance.
The light of winter, pure and bright,
Guides us through the longest night.

Hope ignites with each new dawn,
In winter's heart, we are reborn.
Through the chill, our spirits soar,
In the light of winter, we explore.

Dances of the Cold

Whispers of frost on winter's breath,
Swaying trees in silent depth.
Moonlight casts a silver glow,
Dancing shadows where chill winds blow.

Snowflakes twirl in a gleeful spin,
Nature's rhythm, a soft violin.
Footprints trace the secrets told,
In the quiet, the world unfolds.

Icicles hang like jeweled lights,
Adorning the eaves of winter nights.
Frosted whispers beckon us near,
In this silence, we find no fear.

Crystalline paths under starry skies,
Breath of winter, a soft reprise.
With every step, a story unfolds,
In dances serene, the heart beholds.

So let us dance in the cold's embrace,
Finding warmth in this gentle space.
With joy and laughter, let spirits soar,
In winter's ball, forevermore.

Ethereal White Embrace

Softly falls the gentle snow,
Draping earth in purest glow.
A blanket of peace, soft and light,
Whispers dreams on the edge of night.

Underneath the vast, bright sky,
Snowflakes twinkle as they sigh.
A world transformed in quiet grace,
Nature's tender, warm embrace.

Footprints lead through fields of white,
A journey crafted in soft delight.
Branches bow with weightless frost,
In ethereal beauty, we find what's lost.

Hope dances on a winter breeze,
Carried softly among the trees.
In the chill, hearts learn to rhyme,
With the pulse of the changing time.

Wrapped in silence, find your place,
Within the touch of winter's face.
In the flurry, feel love trace,
A tapestry of the white embrace.

Shimmering Nightfall

Golden sun bids the day goodbye,
Stars awaken in the twilight sky.
Shadows stretch on fields of light,
As whispers weave through oncoming night.

Moonrise paints the world anew,
Marking paths with silver hue.
In the hush, dreams begin to soar,
Night unfurls its velvet door.

Crickets serenade the dark,
While owls hoot their haunting lark.
Rustling leaves in gentle flight,
Nature sways in sweet delight.

Time slows down in velvet wraps,
As the world with magic laps.
In the quiet, secrets call,
Underneath the stars, we fall.

Embrace the wonders of this hour,
Where the night reveals its power.
In shimmering dusk, let hearts ignite,
And dance through the canvas of night.

Crystal Veils of Serenity

Morning dew on petals laid,
Whispers of a new day made.
Sunrise breaks with golden threads,
Spreading warmth where silence treads.

Gentle breezes weave through trees,
Bringing scents of peaceful ease.
Rippling waters softly sing,
In harmony with everything.

Clouds drift by with tender grace,
Adorning the vast, boundless space.
Nature's canvas, soft and bright,
Painted gently in morning light.

Crystal veils that shimmer wide,
Holding dreams that gently bide.
In stillness, hearts begin to grow,
Finding serenity in the flow.

So breathe in this lovely sight,
Let your spirit take to flight.
In nature's arms, find solace here,
In crystal veils, all things are clear.

Milton Keynes UK
Ingram Content Group UK Ltd.
UKHW010232111224
452348UK00011B/695